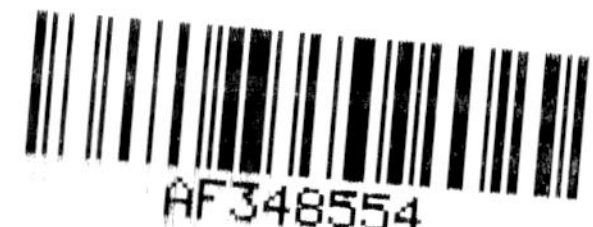

THE DESIGN

THE DESIGN

In case of loss, Please return to: